See the Sights!

Jane Penrose

Contents

Special structures	page 5
Stopping the topple	page 6
Big wheels	page 8
The wrong shade	page 10
Meet Big Ben	page 12
A bumpy ride	page 14
Secrets of the stones	page 16
White wonder	page 18
Record-smashing wall	page 20
The next big thing	page 22
Glossary/Index	page 23

Mini, Macro and Micro World!

Hello. My name is **Mini Marvel**. My dad **Macro Marvel** and I invented **Micro World**. This is the book that inspired us to make the **Wonders of the World** zone.

This page is for an adult to read to you.

Did you know?

Words in the glossary are in alphabetical order to help you find what you want.

Glossary

abseiling	using ropes to lower yourself down
lead	a soft but heavy metallic substance
marble	a hard stone that can be polished to make it very shiny
performing arts	arts that are performed, like drama, music and dance
wreckage	the parts of something that has been destroyed

Joke

Question: What does the Statue of Liberty stand for?

Answer: Because it can't sit down!

Mini's Top Spot

Using the contents, can you find which page you can read about this topic on?

Meet Big Ben

Which heading in the contents are you most interested in?

Before you read

Sound checker
Sounds to remember when you are reading this book.

gh are ear ere ei
ey eigh aigh

Word alert
Blend the sounds. Remember the sounds you have practised.

enou**gh**   c**are**fully   w**ear**
wh**ere**   abs**ei**ling   th**ey**
w**eigh**ts   str**aigh**tened

Into the zone
- Do you know any famous landmarks in other countries?

Special structures

We're going to find out about some of the world's most amazing landmarks.

This **performing arts** centre looks like sails on a boat!

Stopping the topple

This tower in Italy leans to one side because the soil it stands on is not firm enough.

56 m

Different engineers have tried to stop movement in the soil. They aimed to prevent the tower from toppling towards the ground.

Some engineers stacked **lead** weights on one side and drilled away soil. This straightened the tower by 48 cm.

Big wheels

The London Eye towers above everything around it. From it, 800 passengers can see across London in all directions.

The London Eye is not the city's first big wheel – the Great Wheel was constructed in 1894.

The Great Wheel was powered by steam, made by burning fuel.

The wrong shade

The Statue of Liberty in America was not always green. The copper that it is made from was once shiny and amber. Copper turns green when in contact with water and air.

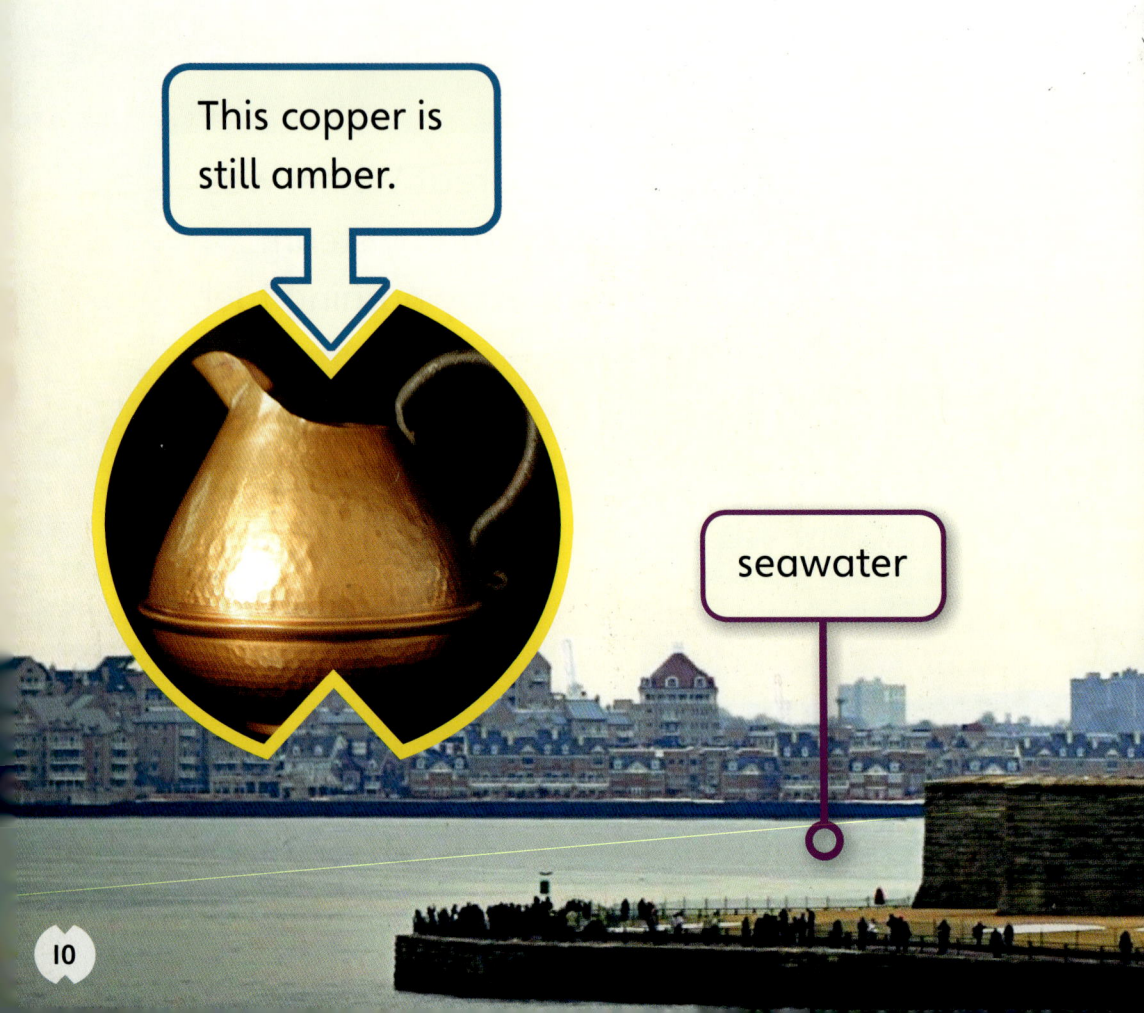

This copper is still amber.

seawater

Meet Big Ben

Big Ben is the bell inside this clock tower in London. People who can bear to stand in the tower when the bell rings wear earplugs – it's as loud as a jet!

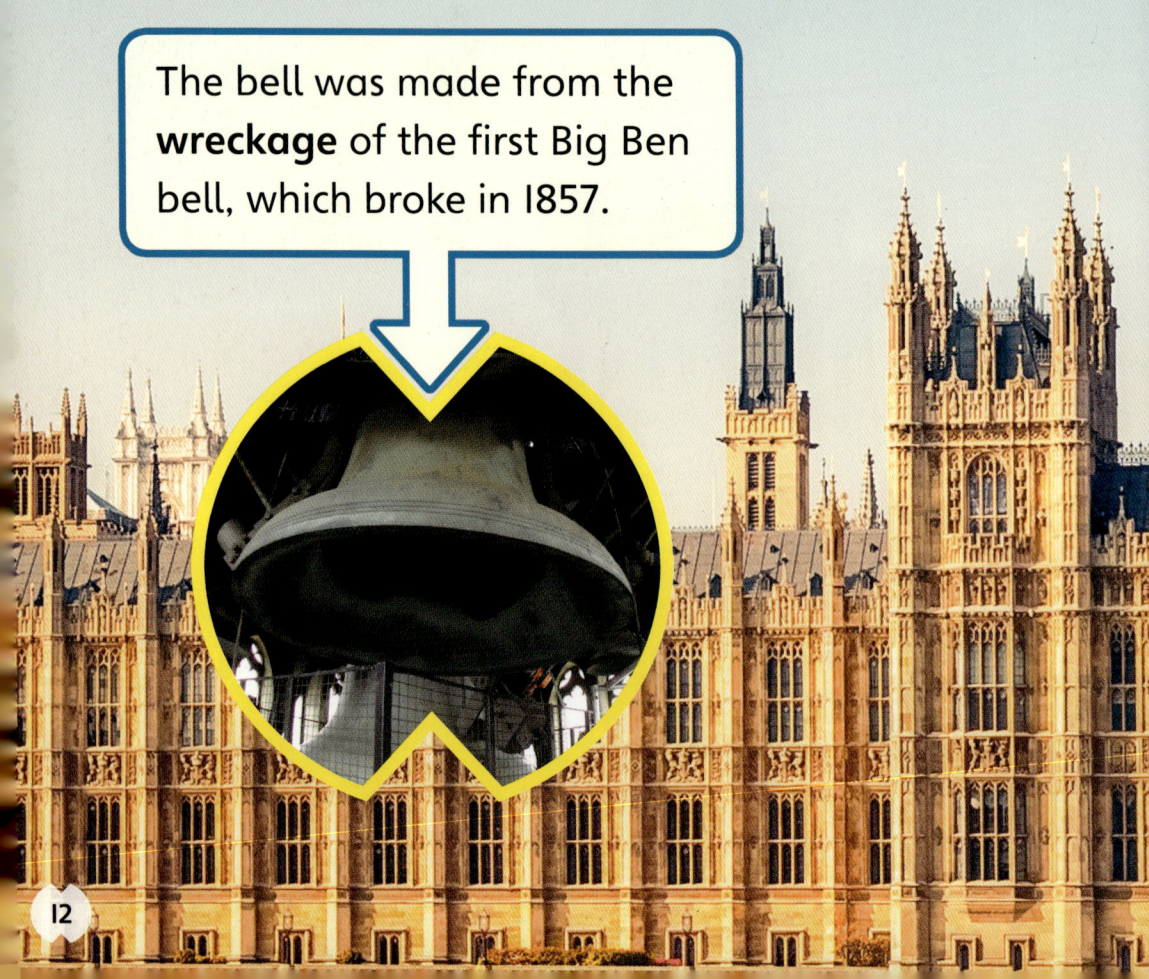

The bell was made from the **wreckage** of the first Big Ben bell, which broke in 1857.

A bumpy ride

The staircase of the Eiffel Tower in France has 1665 steps from top to bottom. In 1923, a man dared to cycle down the steps from the first floor. What a hero!

Painting the tower is a tough job. The painters take 18 months to finish, moving about by **abseiling**.

The tower used to be painted red.

Secrets of the stones

Stonehenge is in the UK. No one is sure why it was made over 4000 years ago or how the stones were moved into place. The biggest stones weigh as much as 4 double-decker buses – enough to make anyone huff and puff!

The stones might have been rolled on logs.

stone circle

White wonder

The Taj Mahal was made nearly 400 years ago. It is covered in white **marble**, which 1000 elephants helped to drag to the site. The landmark is so special it has been called a Wonder of the World.

The structure was made so carefully, it took a total of 22 years before it was finished!

Record-smashing wall

The Great Wall of China is the longest man-made structure on Earth. It is over 9 times as long as the UK! It was made to defend an empire.

The wall snakes across hills and through valleys.

The next big thing

Do you have an idea for a landmark of the future? You could train to become a designer and bring your idea to life!

Glossary

abseiling	using ropes to lower yourself down
lead	a soft but heavy metallic substance
marble	a hard stone that can be polished to make it very shiny
performing arts	arts that are performed, like drama, music and dance
wreckage	the parts of something that has been destroyed

Index

colour	10, 15
copper	10
engineers	6–7
size	16, 20
stone	16–17, 18
tower	6–7, 12–13, 14–15
wheel	8–9

Now you have read ...
See the Sights!

Take a closer look

Read the amazing facts about different landmarks and match each one to the correct picture:

Which landmark ...
... was built with the help of elephants?
... came close to toppling over?
... has changed colour from orange to green?
... has 1165 steps to climb?

Thinking time

Which landmark would you most like to visit?
Explain why you have chosen it.